From Me to You
The Key to a Romantic Relationship

From the lessons of Avraham Lifshitz

By Mazal Lifshitz

From the lessons of
Avraham Lifshitz

From Me to You
The Key to a Romantic Relationship

By Mazal Lifshitz

The man's self-improvement in a romantic relationship
is the **manhood** that is within him
And the woman's self-improvement
is the **femininity** that is within her

The man's need in a romantic relationship is
importance
And the woman's need is
belonging

Mazal Lifshitz

From Me to You

The Key to a Romantic Relationship

From the lessons of Avraham Lifshitz

Senior Editors & Producers: Contento
Collection and editing: Mazal Lifshitz
Editing: Sybil Kaplan
Illustrations: Amir Lifshitz
Cover illustration: Amir Lifshitz
Translated by: Lilach Shahar
Design: Liliya Lev Ari
Proofing: Tal Rivkah Goutta

Copyright © 2015 Contento, Avraham and Mazal Lifshitz

All rights reserved. No part of this book may be translated, reproduced, stored in a retrieval system or transmitted, in any form or by any means, electronic, photocopying, recording or otherwise, without prior permission in writing from the author and publisher.

ISBN: 978-965-550-470-5
International sole distributor: Contento
22 Isserles Street, 6701435, Tel Aviv, Israel
www.ContentoNow.com

Table of Contents

Preface 11

Introduction 13

Chapter One – The First Creation – Human Ego 17

The Creation of Man ; Eve ; Human Ego ; A Supportive Environment

Chapter Two - The Second Creation - Sexual Ego ... 35

Sexual Ego ; Male ; The Romantic Relationship ; The Fable of the Candle ; The Keys ; The Importance of the Man ; Belonging ; King Solomon ; Food for Femininity ; The Fable of the Table, Tableware, and Food ; The Right Sexual Connection ; Symbols in the Subconscious

Chapter Three - The Structure of the Woman's Soul ... 73

The Structure of the Woman's Soul ; Serving Traits ; Essential Traits of the Woman ; Living Childishness ; Optimism ; Love ; Fable – The Glass and the Water ; Femininity – Worldly Essence ; Living Feminine ; Motherhood – An Acquired Spiritual Trait ; Wittiness – An Acquired Worldly Mental Trait ; Wisdom ; Living as Wittiness ; A Charming Weakness ; The Fable of the Bottle and the Glass ; Wittiness – A Charming Weakness ; What is Femininity? ; The Fable of the Flower

Poem of the Path 118

Be thankful for what you have

And what you do not have will be fulfilled

Approbation from Rabbi Shmuel Eliyahu *Shlita*

The chief rabbi of the holy city of Tzfat

Rabbi Isaac Luria (of blessed memory) wrote that it is appropriate for everyone to first say the prayer "here I love each and every one from Israel with all my heart and soul" and in this way the gates of heaven will open up to him and his prayer might be heard.

Improving one's virtues is measured mainly in the relationships between a man and his fellow man and woman. Correct relations are not just proper manners, they are mainly made up of a true "love of Israel."

Rabbi Isaac Luria (of blessed memory) teaches us that having the right virtues is like having the "key" to "the gates of heaven." We must be aware that there are rules to keys—when they are in the right amount, precise, and appropriately directed—even the narrowest key will open heavy gates and metal locks; when they are inappropriately directed—the gate will not be opened by them ever, only heavy hammers and a huge amount of effort might possibly break a path through for them while creating much destruction.

From Me to You

This is what our blessed rabbis have said since "Love your friend as you love yourself" is the key to the whole Torah. On it depend all of the virtues, and upon the virtues everything depends.

A huge blessing to those working on improving their virtues according to the path led by Avraham and his book. May they be blessed from the uppermost heavens "so that all the peoples of the earth may come to know that the name of God is your name and they shall fear you."

Shmuel Eliyahu

Preface

Dear women,

I turn to each and every one of you out of a great understanding of the importance of building a Jewish home. How great is the importance of a man and woman who build the Jewish home!

The material I have written in this book comes out of my dear husband's enormous knowledge. My dear husband has collected the knowledge with his vast wisdom, his healthy perception, and his great sensitivity toward others.

Already in his childhood, he had a deep longing and a strong inner urge for understanding the soul of man. Over a large number of years of deep and healthy observation of human beings and with love for his fellow man, he accumulated more and more knowledge, which was passed on in courses that provided answers to life's questions.

However, I will not be able to pass on all of the material. There is simply too much, encompassing all areas of life.

Within the vast amount of material, I have discovered keys, which, if we use them correctly, will allow us to open the doors to a world that is concealed from us. We will be able to get closer to ourselves and closer to our children. We will be able to connect in our romantic relationships as man and woman. We will find out how to be fitting vessels in building an abode in the physical world for the Creator of the universe.

I chose to write about one key, **the key to a romantic relationship**, a key that is very close to my heart.

Out of great love, it is my desire, as a woman, to pass on to you, the women, the key to a romantic relationship, so that you will be able to realize your important role, to build your personal temple, to build the sacred of the sacred, which is your romantic relationship.

At this exciting opportunity, I offer a tremendous prayer of thanks to the Creator of the universe for allowing me, while writing this book, to experience the vast grace and feel the love of God.

I believe that each and every one of you will be able to assimilate the knowledge imparted through this book and use it in your own couple relationship.

May we very soon be granted the right to burst forth with drums and dancing, to bring about our personal salvation, which will lead to the general salvation.

It was thanks to righteous women who were redeemed, and it is thanks to them that we will be redeemed.

Mazal Lifshitz

Introduction

Romantic Relationship

One of the basic things in a romantic relationships is giving.

A man and a woman in a couple relationship give in different ways due to the sexual ego.

"Male and female he created them." (Genesis 1: 27)

In order for a couple to connect on all levels of the couple relationship, they must merge.

How does this happen?

When there is correct giving in a romantic relationship, there is merging.

The sexual ego must be in a merged state.

The female is the vessel, she is the receiver.

When the male pours into the female, the female feels emotionally full.

Now she can contain the male within her.

This is called merging, being one within the sexual ego.

When there is merging in the sexual ego, a great power is created.

To compel the human ego to want to merge, means to want to give.

From Me to You

How does this take place?

When the word "couple" is written with cursive Hebrew letters, it takes on a symmetrical appearance- זוג: *zayin* on the right, *vav* in the middle, and *gimmel* on the left. When you take out the *vav* in the middle, the *zayin* and *gimmel*, mirror images, come together to form a heart.

Then you turn into one.

The letter *vav* is the condition in the couple's romantic relationship – "If you give to me, I will give to you."

The condition creates a barrier between the two partners; when there is no barrier in the heart, they turn into one – in the human ego.

When the man and the woman are linked within the sexual ego and connected as well within the human ego, then together they are a whole.

Introduction

When you remove the conditional from the relationship you turn into one heart

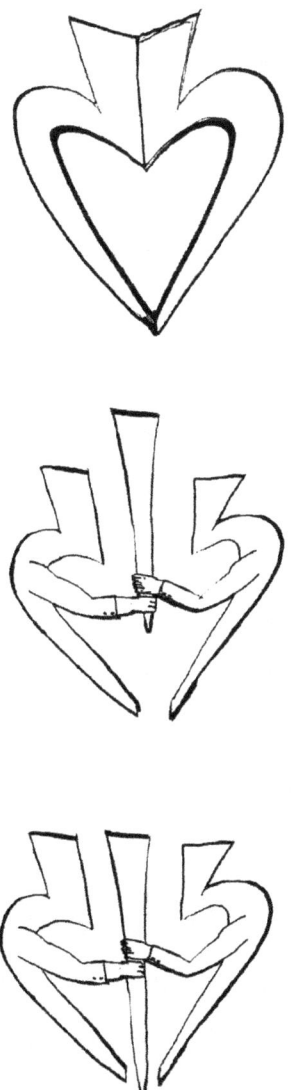

Chapter One

The First Creation Human Ego

Love – The highest spiritual awareness

You arrive at love through giving

Falling in love is material and love is spiritual

The Creation of Man

Preface

Let us try to understand the creation of man, the most important creation. In order to understand this we must go way… way… way…way… back in time.

"So God created humankind in his image, in the image of God He created them; male and female He created them." (Genesis 1: 27)

We can see that we have two creations, two basic primary creations:

our basis for existing.

our basis for realization.

First creation:

"So God created humankind in his image…"

This is the creation of Adam and Eve.

We will call this human ego.

Second creation:

"Male and female he created them."

We will call this sexual ego.

Thus, there are two creations – human ego and sexual ego.

Eve

Before I begin to write about the first creation, I would like to explain to you why I wrote the name Eve despite the fact that she does not appear explicitly in the passage *"Let us make man in our image."*

It is true, the word Eve does not appear, yet it appears in a hidden way.

How?

Eve is a Creation

Hashem created man, and so man is a creation.

Hashem took a rib from the man and created Eve.

Hence, Eve is a creation.

For example, everything that is made of wood will be wood.

Because Eve is created from the man, she is man.

Human Ego

We have named the first creation "Human Ego."

What is human ego?
Ego is a type of I.
Human ego means I am human, which is the human in man.

To work on humanity is the improvement of one's virtues, in society, in the family, and in a romantic relationship.
In the human ego, the man and the woman are similar but not identical.
What does that mean – similar but not identical?
In order for you to understand the depth of the matter, we will take a look at our sources from Genesis:
"So the Lord God caused the man to fall into a deep sleep; and while he was sleeping, he took one of the man's ribs and then closed up the place with flesh." (Genesis 2, 21)

The Free Rib

Hashem caused the man to fall asleep, then took from him one of his ribs.
What is this same rib that *Hashem* took?
It is the free rib that is located between the chest and the stomach – the central area.

In what ways are man and woman similar?
And in what ways are man and woman not identical?

To answer this, we must go into more detail.

Division of Man

Hashem created man from four central parts: head, chest, stomach, and pelvis.
Each part has its own symbolism.
The head symbolizes thinking, efficiency.
The chest symbolizes innate emotions.
The stomach symbolizes acquired sensations.
The pelvis symbolizes urges, aggression.

Full Functioning

Eve was built from man's free rib, which is located between the chest and the stomach, the central area, because she was built from the rib whose location is in the central area; this is her strong place. From this, we understand that Eve received the emotions and sensations that are in the central area, with full functionality.

Eve – Experience
(In Hebrew: *Chava – Chavaya* – חוה - חוויה)

Because Eve received the emotions and sensations with

full functionality, we can say that Eve received the area of experience in life.

Thus, the name *Chava* (Eve) is from the Hebrew word *Chavaya* (experience). Eve experienced life.

The Man was Left

Man, after one of his ribs was taken from him, was left with a weakened central area, meaning that he was left with weakened emotions and sensations.

Women, now you will be able to see the ways in which the man and the woman are similar and in what ways they are not identical.

Similar

Man and woman are similar in these traits. They both have the same traits: thinking, efficiency, emotions, sensations and urges.

Not Identical

Man and woman are not identical in these traits. Woman's primary traits are emotions and sensations. Her secondary traits are thinking, efficiency, and urges.

In man, it is the opposite.

From Me to You

Man's primary traits are thinking, efficiency, and urges. His secondary traits are emotions and sensations.
Dear women, after you have understood and received such a precious treasure from the Creator of the universe, what is now left is to thank the Creator of the universe.

You have received the world of emotions with full functionality, the ability to feel life's heartbeat,
the ability to experience life.
The question that arises is, did you receive this solely for yourselves?
We will return to our sources and look at the book of Genesis.
*The Lord God said, "It is not good for the man to be alone. I will make **a help suitable for him**."* (Genesis 2, 18)
When we look at the first line in the passage, the question that arises is, what does man need to do so that he will not be alone?

Wedding

One of the most important roles that man received was to marry his woman and cherish her. In performing the ritual circumcision, he has entered the covenant of our father Abraham. For this reason, when he cherishes the woman, he brings her into Abraham's covenant.

In the second line of the passage, we see *"**help suitable for him**."*

Help suitable for him *(in Hebrew: "**a help that is against him**")* – as if she is against him, but the woman's role is to **help** her man in his weak areas, which are emotions and sensations.

Women, now you can understand that your emotional center is the **helping** tool for your man, meaning, to help your man remove the foreskin from his heart, despite the fact that sometimes it will seem **as if it is against him**.

Dear women, you should know that the man's self-improvement of his virtues is in the human ego.
Therefore, your man finds it difficult to express weaknesses, to express desires, to express feelings, and this is his job.

In you, the women, your emotional center has full functionality, and so, this should be your nature.

We will focus on the inner point of a romantic relationship. The question that arises is:
What is the aim of the romantic relationship in the human ego?
The aim is to reach catharsis, to *"become one flesh."* (Genesis 2, 24)

They Want the Same Thing

As equal human beings in the human ego, both man and woman want the same thing.
They both want good human relations.
They both want emotional openness, emotional flow.
They both want love.

Being One

Both man and woman have a deep inner need that wants to feel the emotional merging,
the human merging.
They want to be one in the human ego.

How is this accomplished?
In a romantic relationship, there is a need to work all of the time. There is a need for openness, a need for improvement of one's virtues, a need to know how to yield, how to forgive, and how to be considerate.
To know that in a romantic relationship, there is no such thing as "I deserve it," because I am who I am.

The Laws of Nature

Let us learn something important from the laws of nature. Nature is built in such a way, that when I want something to grow, I need to invest, so that there will be growth.

So it is in a romantic relationship

Each one wants to receive from the other.

In order to receive, one has to invest in the other,

and only in this way, will there be growth because this is the law of nature.

Caring

This is human expression that opens the heart.

It is very important in a romantic relationship that there will be caring for one another.

When caring is felt, it creates a desire to give to one another.

When caring is felt, it creates intimacy, it creates a strong emotional connection, it creates belonging.

In addition to this, it is very important that there will be two additional things in the romantic relationship:

1. Respect for one another.
2. Support for one another.

The man and the woman want these things equally, yet the road is not identical.

You are the woman!
The road to reaching your man's heart is very important. If you, as a woman, respect your man, despite his weaknesses, and support his weaknesses with a lot of encouragement, your man will respect you and support your weaknesses and your difficulties.

Purification of Virtues

When you get to a point in a romantic relationship, where the human attributes are equally pure, they become similar.
If we connect the man's human attributes together with the woman's, we will see that they appear as one.
A full match is created between the man and the woman in the human ego.
Emotional openness is created, as well as emotional flow. Love of acceptance and giving is created.
A connection in the human ego is made, of *"becom[ing] one flesh."*

A Supportive Environment

One of the most important things that we are supposed to do in life is to change. In order for us to change, we need to feel that we are not threatened.

In order for us to feel that we have a supportive environment in our romantic relationship, it is very important that we know how to speak and that we know how to listen.

Proper speaking in a romantic relationship enables emotional openness and enables us to open our hearts, so that both partners are able to share with one another the deep things that are within them.

How do we speak?

1. **Speak positively.**

Speak with words that widen the heart. Many times, we are speaking in a positive conversation, but we insert negative words into the conversation. The subconscious receives the negative, and this causes a contracting, and then we are unable to open up emotionally.

2. **Speak in the first person.**

When we speak in the second person, "You!" people immediately defend themselves.

Usually when we are defending ourselves, we react with aggression.

3. Do not criticize.

Criticism is a borrowed word from the technical world. In the technical world, criticism means comparison between a product and a plan.

We borrow criticism from the technical world into the social world.

When I see something that is not clear to me and react immediately, that is aggression.

If I have found out what the plan is, and I have compared it to the product, then I can criticize and state my opinion. This is constructive criticism.

An additional condition is needed, which is that I am personally involved.

For example, the woman sees her husband enter the house with his shoes covered with mud; the woman is angry and criticizes him for it. This is not criticism, it is aggression. Why?

The woman is missing a plan by which she can criticize him. The woman saw a product – her husband entering with mud on his shoes.

But she is supposed to ask him about the plan. Perhaps the husband will tell her that he had to enter the house quickly and then the product and plan will match.

4. Do not blame.

Blaming causes a feeling of helplessness, the feeling that my fate has been sealed without a trial.

Now, what I need to do is convince that it is not me.

5. Do not judge.

People do not like to be judged.

People do not like it when someone makes himself the judge without their permission, and tells them,

"It is okay" and "It is not okay."

6. Do not educate.

A person who educates puts him or herself above.

The right kind of communication between adults is equality.

One does not educate the other.

A parent educates his child because it is his or her role.

A teacher educates because it is his or her role.

7. Do not teach.

Nobody likes to be taught if:

1. He did not ask to be taught.
2. The teacher did not ask the learner's permission to teach.

8. Do not speak in generalizations.

It is very important, especially in romantic relationships,

not to speak in generalizations; one should speak in details.

For example, if the woman tells her husband, "I am disappointed in you," this is a general statement which the husband cannot do anything with, it only lowers his confidence.

If the woman says, "I am disappointed in you because this morning I waited to hear good-morning from you." Now, the husband can understand what he can correct in his behavior.

9. Do not begin a sentence with a question.

In interpersonal communication, we do not begin a sentence with a question. This causes the other person to justify himself.

For example, if you ask your husband "Why didn't you call?"

Your husband will feel that you are complaining to him.

All he has left to do is to justify himself.

Of course, he does not like it.

But, if you tell him "I waited for your call," your husband can open his heart and explain to you at length what happened.

10. Don't talk in absolute, total terms.

It is not permitted to speak, in interpersonal relations, in absolute terms, such as "You're always angry," "You never help me."

When we speak in this way, we are essentially placing a stamp on the other.

Now, he will never be able to change. There is a stamp on him.

11. Do not invalidate.

People become very angry when they are invalidated.

For example, "No, that's not true," "You don't know."

A block is created; there is no way of opening up.

Conclusion

People can change only in a supportive environment.

Chapter Two

The Second Creation
Sexual Ego

The more the man is more of a man and
the woman is more of a woman,
the stronger the force of life between them will be.

Communication is the central motif
in a romantic relationship.

Sexual Ego

We will move on to the second creation: *"Male and female he created them."* (Genesis 1, 27)

The creation of the sexual ego, the excitement in life, the vitality of life.

What do we see in the passage?

Male and female – there are two.
Created – there is one.
Them – many.

We can see here, one creation is divided into two.

This means that each one is half of the whole; each one is 50%, together they are 100%.

Male and female are two reversed halves.

In order to understand the reversal that is between them, there is a need to understand first: What is male? And what is female?

From Me to You

Male

Weapon

The male is like a weapon. It is divided in two.
We will take, for example, the classic weapon, a bow and arrow.
They are one, yet they act differently.

The male is divided in two.
Plus male = arrow.
Minus male = bow.
They are one. Yet they act differently.

What are the traits of an arrow?
Straightforward, breaks through, conquers, penetrative, splitting, bold, achiever, extrovert, stuck on the goal, inconsiderate of his surroundings, etc.

Dear women, I would like for you to take a look at our sources and see what is hiding in the passages from the book of Genesis:

First passage:
"So God created mankind in his own image, in the image of God he created them; **male and female he created them***."*
(Genesis 1, 27)

Second Passage:
*"God blessed them and said to them, "Be fruitful and multiply; fill the earth and **conquer** it"."* (Genesis 1, 28)

Women, what do we see?

In the first passage, we can see the creation of the sexual ego.

In the second passage, we see the first *mitzvah* in the Torah, the *mitzvah* to be fruitful and multiply.

In the same passage, we see the words, **conquer** it.

What do the words "conquer it" tell us?

A continuation of the command.

The man and woman are equally obligated,
but the man is the leader.

Why?

He is the male. He is the one who breaks through, he is the initiator, the active one.

Hence, man's way is to conquer and attack.

Women, if this trait appears in the book of Genesis, then it appears that it is a very significant trait for us.

The question that arises is – why is it so significant?

From nature's point of view, the woman is attracted to a plus male, her interest is to secure strong offspring.

How does this happen?

When the male conquers the female, meaning, uses the trait of the arrow, the woman feels the power, the validity of her husband, she trusts him, she can let go. She can lose control.

Now, she feels that she is his female, and then she becomes a good vessel for creating offspring that are of higher quality, genetically speaking.

Women, these are things that are rooted deeply within, in our genes, they are part of us. They are a part of creation.

Memory
(In Hebrew, the word memory is spelled the same as the word male זכר.)

A male wants to be remembered, it is in his genes, therefore he sows a seed.

What will sprout is his memory.

Male and Female

The male is active, he is the conqueror.

He sows the seed (in Hebrew, seed is spelled the same as sperm), his genes, in the female.

The female is like the soil, she protects the seed and makes sure it will sprout.

Male – remember.

Female – protect.

Remember and protect leads me to *Shabbat* candles.

What is the relation? There is a relation!

Shabbat candles

The woman lights holy *Shabbat* candles, lights that remember and protect.

Remember – male. Protect – female.

There is a huge hint here – the connection between a male and female on the day of *Shabbat*.

From here, we can understand the great importance of the pairing of the man and woman on the holy *Shabbat*.

What is a minus male?

A minus male has the traits of the bow.

What are the traits of the bow?

The bow is rounded, flexible.

It does not appear threatening; it is far from the location of the event.

The bow and a minus male

The bow sends but stays behind.

So does the minus male. He can teach, explain, but he stays outside.

The bow is round and not threatening.
Such is the minus male —
In your favor, a gentleman, friend, supportive, sheltering, does not appear threatening.

The bow is far away from the event.
Such is the minus male –
non-initiating, passive, far away from where the event takes place.
The man needs to embody both plus male and minus male.

Female

Female – in Hebrew, *nekeva*, נקבה, comes from the Hebrew word for piercing or hole, *nekev*, נקב.
The essence of the piercing is the desire to become full.
Nekeva – two words.
Nekev – ba (in Hebrew, *ba* means "in her")
Thus, she wants to become full like a piercing.

Women, after you have understood the meaning of male and the meaning of female, now you can understand the reversal that exists between them.
The male wants to fill.
He is the one who is active, breaks through, conquers, therefore he sows a seed.
The female wants to become full,

she is passive,

she is a vessel that wants to become full.

She protects and makes sure that the seed will sprout.

I will give an example of a reversed expression.

Man and woman both want a hug.

Their desires are similar, but the expression is reversed.

The man wants to hug,

and the woman wants to feel hugged.

The Romantic Relationship

In a romantic relationship, there is a need for exciting emotions.

Why?

We received this trait back from when we were fetuses.

In order for you to understand the whole subject, I would like to expand the subject and go into more detail.

The Fetus in the Womb

When the fetus is in the womb, it is in a state of two opposites. On one hand, the whole fetus is wrapped inside the womb, and this makes it feel entirely protected; therefore, it has security in the womb.

On the other hand, the fetus is floating around in amniotic fluid, it has no stability; with every move the mother makes it is being shaken.

The floating, the shaking, and the movements make it feel excitement.

Therefore a human being needs these two conditions: security and excitement.

How does a human being conduct himself in life with these two conditions?

What happens in the end of the process of puberty in a human, is that the human splits the two needs.

Security joins the human being that is within him or her.

Excitement joins the masculinity or femininity – the sexual ego.

When the human being builds a family, the two parts search for their nourishment.

Where will the human being receive this?

The security he or she will receive from his or her family.

The excitement he or she will receive from his or her romantic relationship.

A romantic relationship and family are two opposite things.

On one hand, the romantic relationship and the family are dependent on one another.

On the other hand, the family, which is the security, annihilates the excitement in the romantic relationship.

In order to demonstrate these, I will bring in my dear husband's fable.

The Fable of the Candle

The symbol of the romantic relationship in a candle is the wick.
The symbol of the family in a candle is the flame.
The flame sits on the wick.
We can see that on the one hand, they are dependent on each other.
On the other hand, the flame annihilates the wick.
In order for the flame not to annihilate the wick, the wick needs to renew itself all the time.

So it is with family and a romantic relationship

On one hand, there is dependence upon one another; on the other hand, the family annihilates the romantic relationship.
Why?

Family is made up of heavy things, such as determination, responsibility, good judgment, debts, educating the children, and so on…
A romantic relationship is emotional excitement.
There is a need for vitality; therefore there is a constant need to renew and be renewed.

What do we do?
We must break the routine.
One of the simple things that can be done in a romantic relationship is to surprise one another.
Surprise is renewal.
It breaks the routine and creates emotional excitement.

The family seeks security; a romantic relationship seeks exciting emotions.
How do we combine these two together?
An additional thing that causes emotional excitement in a romantic relationship is the masculine behavior toward the feminine and the feminine behavior toward the masculine.

This is a very important thing that the man and woman need to know and bring into the romantic relationship.

The Burning of Life

Excitement in a romantic relationship is the fuel that preserves the burning of life. The excitement of a romantic relationship provides the strength to deal with the burden of the family.
Women, in our period in time, there is a greater need for expressing exciting emotions.
Why?

Once

In previous periods in time, life was very much based on survival.

There was a great need for security. There was no room for exciting emotions.

It was not acceptable for a woman to desire emotional excitement from her husband.

Today

The times are changing, we are moving into a spiritual period in time.

In a spiritual period of time, there is the energy of love.

Therefore, there is a need to express love in the human ego and there is a need to express intimate love in the sexual ego.

"And they became one flesh"

In a spiritual period in time, there is a need for realizing the romantic relationship as a whole.

Love in the human ego, excitement in the sexual ego, allow for us to connect and realize, in our romantic relationships.

"And they became one flesh"

The Sexual ego

The Keys

Dear women,

Up until now, I have explained to you in a general way, about the second creation – the sexual ego.

Now, it is time to give you two very precious keys.
I give you the keys with love so that you can use them.
The first key we will call **importance**.
The second key we will call **belonging**.

Please know that when the man receives importance from his woman, he feels that he is "her man."

When the woman receives belonging from her man, she feels the "femininity" that is in her.

The Importance of the Man

One of the things you need to know as a woman, is to give your man importance.

A man who does not feel importance from his wife, loses his confidence in the romantic relationship.

In order for you to understand this in an in-depth way, we will return to our sources.

The primary genes

Because man was created on the last day of the creation, he contains everything that was created before him; it can be said that man contains within him the basic primary male genes of the animals that were created before him.

You can see this in nature.

The Period of Courtship in Nature

If we take a look at nature during the period of courtship that takes place between animals, we can see that the males behave very violently.

For example, males from the deer family grow horns on their heads like trees, sharp as knives.

With them, they butt into one another, and like in war,

there are wounded and even casualties.
You are probably asking, what is this war for?

The male in nature wants to be the strongest,
he wants to be the most important,
he wants to be an Alpha male.
In nature, the male that beats all the other males is the strongest male, the most important male in the herd, therefore, he is chosen as the Alpha male in the herd.

Head of the Herd

When the male becomes the Alpha male in the herd, the females in the herd will come and unite with him; he will be the father of their next generation of offspring.
Therefore, he becomes the head of the heard, a head that cares for all.

That is the Way it is with Men

Every man wants to feel, with his woman, that he is her Alpha male.
The man feels this not in his wit or in his feelings; this is a deep need, that he has as part of his basic instincts; it is in his genes.
Women, I will reveal to you the amount of insecurity your man experiences.
In the man's deep feeling, he feels, "If I am not my woman's

Alpha male, then why should I have the security that she will not find another Alpha male?"

The Alpha Male

As human beings we are organized in pairs, therefore, men do not have the need to wrestle among themselves, because in human beings, the woman turns her man into an Alpha male.

In the Distant Past

In the distant past, women had many customs, with which they gave their man importance.

For example, a woman who knew that her husband was returning from work, would wash her husband's feet at the entrance to the house.

In a later period, the woman would greet him with a bowl of water so that he could wash his hands.

Women behaved out of their inner nature. They knew how to give their man importance.

There was a feminine wisdom that came out from inside of them.

They knew how to raise their heads so that he would feel he was the Alpha male.

And what is happening today?

Women, you are right, we are in a different period, but there are still things you can do today and get the same result as you would have before.

A Few Tips:

- Give your husband the feeling that his opinion is important to you.
- Don't take your husband for granted.
- Give your husband the feeling that you appreciate him.

Tips from the kitchen:

You probably know that the most important thing for your man is food. Therefore,

- Always give your husband the first course.
- If important guests are coming, such as father, grandfather, etc., there are some women who serve them first. In this case, give your husband a bigger and more honorable portion.
- If you want to find out whether the food tastes good, always ask your husband first.

Women, there are things you should not do because they take away from your husband's importance.

What are these things?

- Do not compare your man to anyone else.
- Do not cancel out your man. Do not say "no, it's not," "you don't know."
- Do not speak in hints.

For example, "Rivka is so lucky, her husband bought her a car for her birthday."

Instead of hinting, simply ask.

- Do not argue

Arguments begin because of disagreement.
If the argument lasts for more than two sentences, another problem arises – who is right?

What should you do?
Tell your husband – you are right! As you think,
"I think differently."

Here the argument ends, your husband is happy.
In being right,
he feels he is up above,
and when he feels up above, he can give to you.

If your husband tells you that he had a conflict with

another person, and you think your husband is right, then be in his favor.

If you think that the other person is right, it is better to stay silent.

Belonging

What is belonging?

Belonging is intimacy.
It is giving that can be received only from your husband.
It is giving from the masculine to the feminine in acts.
It is looks, compliments, surprises.
It is what are called nutrients for the femininity.

Belonging is one of the most important things for a woman. Why?
There is an improvement of one's virtues here.
Women, you surely remember that the man's self-improvement is by humaneness, and the woman's self-improvement is by femininity.

In Belonging

The woman needs to receive from her husband out of his deep intimate layer, that belongs only to her.
Only then can the woman give to her husband from out of her deep intimate layer, that belongs only to him.
This creates a very strong connection.

King Solomon

Here is some of King Solomon's wisdom.

Why did my dear husband choose King Solomon?

1. King Solomon was the wisest of the wise.
2. He had 1000 women and they were all satisfied.
3. King Solomon, the wisest of the wise, knew the basic principles of a romantic relationship, 3000 years ago. Principles always stay good during all of time; in our day, these principles have been forgotten.

What did King Solomon Say?

"He who finds a wife finds what is good."
(Proverbs 18, line 22)

"I find more bitter than death the woman who is a snare."
(Ecclesiastes 7, line 26)

These two passages are from different books, but there is a relationship between them.

We will divide the first passage into two parts:

Finds a wife – result – **finds what is good**.

We can see that in the first part of the passage, the emphasis is on **the woman**.

When the emphasis is on the woman, this means that the woman must be given to.

What should the woman be given? We will find out later.

We will move on to the word "finds."

What did the man find in the woman?

- When the man turns to the woman,

    He will make her feel that he has found the womanliness in her.

- When the man turns to the woman,

    He must look at her with a look that is as if he just now **found** her.

The Hidden is Revealed

What did the man give to the woman?

He gave her attention.

We will call this food for the womanliness.

What did the man find in the woman?

The man found the womanliness that is within her.

The second part of the passage –

"Finds what is good."

If the man gives the womanliness food,

The woman will feel like a queen,

A queen wants a king, therefore the woman will turn her man into a king.

And then the result – **"Finds what is good."**

The second passage:

Here, too, we will divide the passage into two parts.

- **"I find ... the woman who is a snare"** - result - **"more bitter than death"**

We can find, in the first part of the passage, an emphasis on **I**.

- If the man wants to receive from the woman before he gives to the woman,

The result is - **more bitter than death**.

Dear women,

The key has been revealed.

We will call the key – food for femininity.

Food for Femininity

Dear women,

What is that key that is called food for femininity?

Food for femininity is belonging.

In order for a woman to feel the belonging, she needs three things:

1. To feel courted.
2. To feel loved.
3. To feel desired.

What is Courted?

Every kind of giving from the masculinity to the femininity gives the woman the feeling that she is courted.

For example, if the husband brings his wife a big bouquet of flowers and the woman has not even had time to thank him yet, the husband will take out one sole flower and tell her "this is for the bedroom"…

Now the woman will feel courted.

Another example, if the husband buys his wife a new car, she will be happy and tell all her friends that her husband has a heart of gold. But, the woman will not feel courted. If the husband buys a small colorful scarf and ties it to the key chain and then tells her, "I saw a beautiful scarf, it reminded me of you"…

Now the woman will feel courted.

What is Loved?

There are three things that the woman needs in order to be loved:

1. When the man is near her, he should say things she will love hearing.

For example,

"I cannot be without you,"

"I think about you all the time."

2. When the man is outside of the house he should make the romantic relationship communication with her. In a romantic relationship communication, there is no need for time, organizing, and there is no need for quantity.

Very simply, pick up the phone and say,

"I miss you!"

"You're wonderful"!

"I was just thinking about you!"

A woman feels loved when she is in her husband's head all the time.

3. Emotional excitement - excitement is surprises, doing something that the woman was not expecting.

What is Desired?

A woman who is in a romantic relationship, from a sexual point of view, is in one of the following three conditions:

1. Abandoned.
2. Needed.
3. Desired.

What is abandoned?

When the man is less interested in the woman than she is in him.

Here the woman feels the experience of being abandoned.

What is needed?

When the man wants the woman more than she wants him.

Here the woman feels the experience of being needed.

I am here "by coincidence."

What is desired?

In order for a woman to feel desired, her husband needs to be her man.

What is a man?

A man (in Hebrew, *gever* – גבר) comes from the Hebrew word *gover* – גובר (in English, overcome) which means he overcomes his sexual urges.

But, when the husband sees his woman acting a little bit differently, talking differently or dressing differently, now, he can no longer contain himself:

The Sexual ego

It is because of you... you are to blame...

You made me want you!

This is the only place in a romantic relationship where it is okay to blame, it is even desirable.

When the woman feels she is the cause of her husband's desire, it raises her feminine ego and lets her feel desired.

Three of these conditions: courted, loved, and desired are one unit.

The woman needs all three in order to feel she has received food for her femininity.

Here is a fable by my dear husband. It is a simple fable from life, but it illustrates everything...

The Fable of the Table, Tableware, and Food

When a person comes into a restaurant and wants to eat, he needs a table, tableware, and food.

If he receives a table with a silk tablecloth and scented candles, it will not satisfy him.

If a person receives tableware that is covered with gold, and a crystal plate, it will not satisfy him.

If a person receives the best food, but it is not served esthetically, he will not have an appetite.

Therefore a person needs all three of these things together. Only in this way will he feel satisfied.

The Right Sexual Connection

A Large Gap

Women, you know that a man's natural place is in his lusts, which is the pelvis.

A woman's natural place is in her emotions, which is the chest.

A large gap is created between the man and the woman.

The man wants sex through his urges.

The woman wants sex through her emotions.

What do we do? How do we bridge the gap?

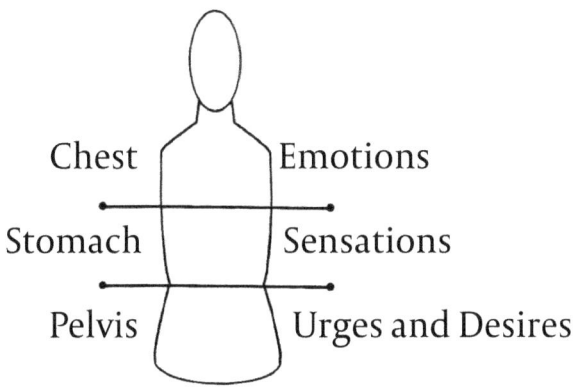

There is a special method.

The man needs to leave his masculinity in his lusts, and raise himself up to the woman's emotions using his humanity, which is the spiritual uterus to the woman's emotions.

She Feels Love

When the woman feels how significant she is in her husband's life...
When she feels her husband's good-heartedness...
When she feels that he cares for her and is in her favor...
When she feels she is inside his spiritual uterus, protected...
When she feels that "near him nothing will happen to me..."

When the woman feels all of this,
she feels that he loves her.
It touches upon her intimate emotions.
Then she can connect with him.

Devoting Oneself

The woman gets security,
she lets herself be devoted to her husband,

to trust him, lean on him.

Now, she can give up her "I."

To Yield

If a woman lowers herself down to her lusts through her humanity, without any intimate emotions,

she will feel that she is in charity and benevolence.

If the woman lowers herself down to her lusts through her femininity,

she will feel like a queen.

Symbols in the Subconscious

Here is another thing from a different and special point of view, how my dear husband sees the symbols of man and woman in the subconscious.

Man

The man's symbol in the subconscious is an upside-down triangle.

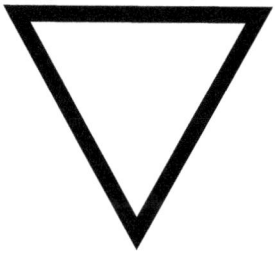

The Structure of the Triangle

If we look at the triangle that represents the man, we will see that the upper part of the triangle is wide and the lower part is narrow.

The upper part represents the shoulder belt, meaning, a man's strength is in extroverted emotions whose source is in the shoulder belt.

The Nape of the Neck

The nape of the neck is the main organ in the shoulder belt, and the qualities it represents are:

Responsibility, protection, firmness, determination, carrying the weight of the livelihood, shelter, belonging, preservation, fighting, and initiation.

Woman

The symbol of the woman in the subconscious is an equilateral triangle:

The Structure of the Triangle

If we look at the triangle that represents the woman, we will see that the lower part of the triangle is wide and the upper part is narrow.

The lower part represents the woman's pelvic belt, meaning, a woman's strength is in her intimate emotions whose source is the pelvis.

The Womb

The womb is the main organ in the pelvis.

The traits it represents are:

softness, mercy, modesty, warmth, giving, creation of life, acceptance, absorption, the experience of life and life's flow.

These traits are the traits that the man in is need of and is attracted to.

It is the woman's role to create an inner home, which represents the traits of the womb.

When the woman correctly implements the traits of the womb and the man correctly implements the traits of the nape of the neck, they create two opposing triangles – the Star of David.

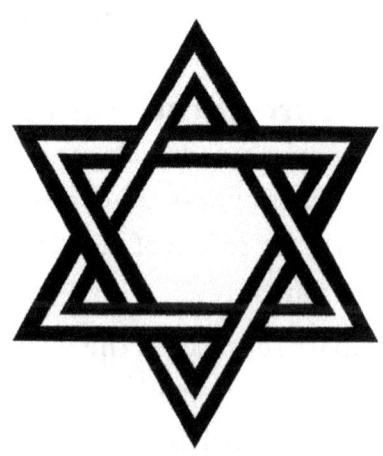

The Star of David

The Star of David stabilizes the shared flow of life.

In it, an inner space is created with six triangles in its circumference: three belonging to the woman and three to the man.

The two upper triangles are the man's; they relate to protection, preservation, shelter, and belonging.

Both of the triangles are on top, therefore, it is very important that you as the woman make sure they stay on top - meaning, that you give your man importance, so that your man, with his shoulders, will be able to protect and shelter you.

The man's lower triangle is the territory; with the help of his territorial need, he anchors himself, he provides the security of an anchor in life.

The two lower triangles are the woman's; they are in the pelvis, and relate to the intimate area of life.

The woman's intimate areas of life are three in number:

1. The bedroom
2. Toiletry
3. The kitchen

These three things are very intimate for a woman.

The husband would be wise to behave with sensitivity in respect to these intimate areas.

From Me to You

Compliments from the husband to the wife will only help.

The woman's upper triangle relates to the soul of the house, meaning, to the woman's excessive wisdom, what is called, woman's wisdom.

The internal space in the Star of David constitutes the heart of the emotional connection that is between them: love, unity, peace, and trust.

It is up to both partners to be familiar with the difference as well as what is equal between them and respect each other.
"Therefore shall a man leave his father and his mother, and shall cleave unto his wife: and they shall be one flesh."
(Genesis 2, 24)

Chapter Three

The Structure of the Woman's Soul

When I hide from life, life searches for me.

Whatever bothers you on the outside, that is your self-improvement inside.

Embarrassment – the fear of revealing what I am hiding.

The Structure of a Woman's Soul

I feel a strong need to share with you my feelings as a woman. I am full of wonder at the material regarding the structure of the woman's soul.

The Magic

I have discovered that there is a special magic in women, a magic she has received from the Creator of the Universe, with which she has the spiritual flexibility to pull out from within her soul a different trait that fits the required need exactly.

Truly magical.

Suddenly she is womanly, tomorrow childish, now charmingly weak, and so on…

The material is written in a deep yet simple way, so that with your wisdom and understanding, you can use the qualities of your soul in life according to the required need.

I will not be able to write out all of the material; the material is built in such a way that there is a need to get into tiny details and deep analysis. There are also tables there where each and every woman, if she wishes to, can find the structure of her soul.

Therefore, I will write for you the essence of the material in a general way, so that you will be able to understand the basic principle of the structure of the woman's soul.

Essence and Serving Traits in the Soul

The structure of a woman's soul is built from two parts:
1. Essence
2. Serving Traits

What is essence?

In order for us to understand what essence is in the structure of a woman's soul, we will divide the essence into two parts:
1. Innate spiritual traits.

These traits are called childish and feminine.

2. The intensity of the traits and their quantity, which is called a receptacle.

We are born with a receptacle. Every woman has a different receptacle.

Essential Traits

The essential traits are experiential, innocent, and dependent traits.

The essential traits are those that give us the experience of life.

Throughout our lives, we can wear out the essential traits because of survival situations; but there is a way to repair and restore the traits to their original size.

Serving Traits

What are Serving Traits?

In order for us to understand what are serving traits in the structure of the woman's soul, here, too, we will divide it into two parts:

1. Traits that we have acquired at the moment of birth These traits are called motherhood and wit.
2. The size of the receptacle that is innate will determine the amount of serving traits that we can acquire.

The serving traits are executive. Serving traits provide work but not joy. They help us match ourselves to the period of time in which we live.

We acquired the serving traits after our birth, through learning, education, observation, under stressful conditions and survival situations.

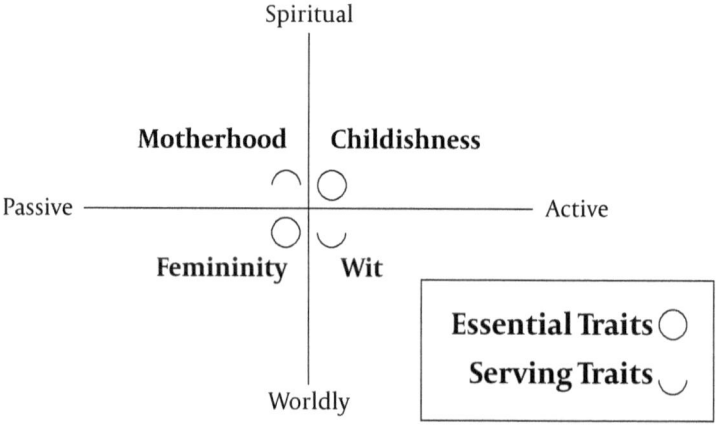

Essential Traits of the Woman

Childish Traits

These are spiritual essential traits, traits that we were born with, they are traits that give us the experience of life.

I would like to elaborate upon the traits so that you will be able to recall and refresh.

What are the childish traits?

Spontaneity, dependence, naivety, lack of boundaries, enthusiasm, dynamism, openness, curiosity, renewal, originality, selfishness, cheerfulness, straightforwardness, mischievousness, optimism, happiness, spiritual flexibility, adventurousness, flow, creativity, joy of life, etc…

In Us as Well

Take a good look at these traits. Are they familiar to you?

Yes, we are all familiar with these traits in our children. Actually, these traits exist or are supposed to exist in our soul as well, even today, when, in terms of our age, we are no longer girls.

Living Childishness

Openness

If we are able to speak openly, mainly in our romantic relationship, and express what we want and what we feel, we will flow emotionally.

When the emotions flow, there is happiness in the heart.

Enthusiasm

When we are enthusiastic about something, we are allowed to express our enthusiasm (within the boundaries of modesty, of course).

We are allowed to be enthusiastic even about the small things in life.

We are all familiar with how we are enthusiastic about every little thing a baby does.

Mischievousness

We can feel good about ourselves, if we feel like singing, dancing, playing, and fooling around with the children.

You can also, if you want to, appear funny, mischievous, gay.

Of course, all of this should be done within the permitted boundaries and by choice.

Renewal

Childishness provides us with the ability to renew ourselves every day anew.

We can wake up in the morning and begin the day with new enthusiasm.

Spiritual Flexibility

Childishness provides us with the spiritual flexibility to change and be changed.

For example, a green branch. When we bend a green branch, the branch is flexible; it will not break.

When we bend a dry branch, it lacks flexibility; it will break.

Optimism

Childishness gives us the ability to start anew after a crisis, to be optimistic and discover that we have, inside of us, the mental powers to start building everything from the beginning.

The Child in Us

Women, it is important that you know, that a child needs two basic things in his life: security and excitement.

Where does this need come from?

The truth is, we received this need when we were in our fetal stage.

When the fetus is in his mother's womb, he or she is in two states, security and excitement.

We will try to understand, why does the fetus feel secure in his mother's womb?

The fetus in the womb is surrounded by very clear boundaries. Boundaries provide security.

Within these boundaries, the fetus feels the heat, the softness of the womb.

He or she feels how the uterus envelops and protects him or her.

The fetus feels that here nothing will happen to me, I am as safe as can be.

Women, there is no greater security than the womb.

Why does the fetus feel excitement in his or her mother's womb?

The fetus in the womb floats around in the amniotic fluid, every step taken by Mom is a fluctuation.

Think now, how many fluctuations does the fetus go through in a day?

A fluctuation is like a swing, it is an experience, it is what is called excitement.

And what happens when Mom coughs? Total loss of control, there are no handles to grab…

Women, now you understand where the child's need for security and excitement come from.

But the question that arises is, how does the child receive the security and excitement?

A child divides into two:

- A minus child
- A plus child

What is a minus child?

A minus child needs unconditional warmth and love.

When he or she receives this, he or she feels security.

But, the need for warmth and love is a passive need, it cannot be realized.

How does a minus child realize his or her need?

In order to realize this need, he or she needs a servant; the servant is called a plus child.

How does a plus child function?

A plus child is active; he or she knows how to make the environment love him or her.

He or she knows how to use excitement, be dramatic, express weaknesses, express emotions, fool around, play, he or she knows how to attract attention.

He or she knows how to receive warmth and love,

And what happens – a minus child feeds off of this.

Love

Women, I would like to write a bit about love.

Love surrounds our whole lives. There is nothing that cannot be placed under the category of love.

We will divide love into two parts – The worldly part and the spiritual part.

And each part divides into two additional parts:

Spiritual

The spiritual that is in the spiritual	Creator
The worldly that is in the spiritual	Creation

Worldly

The spiritual that is in the worldly	Acceptance
The worldly that is in the worldly	Warmth

The worldly that is in the worldly – this is the warmth.

Warmth – in Hebrew: *chom* חום – from the Hebrew word for material, *chomer* חומר.

The warmth is the material part of love that can be realized through the senses.

The spiritual that is in the worldly – acceptance.

Accepting myself as I am, and accepting the other as he is.

The worldly that is in the spiritual – creation.
Loving creation because the creator is in it, loving every human being because he has the divine spark "In God's image he created them," loving man because of the divine spark that is within him.

The spiritual that is in the spiritual – Creator.
The highest love there is, is the spiritual desire in us to connect and merge with the Creator and be one.

Women, we can see that at every age the child receives warmth and love in a different way.

Up to age three

A child needs to receive warmth unconditionally. Warmth is the material part of love. A child can, at this age, grasp love through warmth, through the senses.

Therefore, it is very important to give a child unconditional warmth. Only when a child feels he or she has been given the warmth that he or she needs and feels full, only then will he or she feel security.

Warmth = security.

From age three to seven

A child needs unconditional warmth and acceptance; I am accepted "because I am what I am."

A child needs to feel that even if his or her actions are not right, he or she will continue to be accepted.

It is important to keep on giving the child the feeling that we love you, because you are our child, without relation to your actions.

One of the crucial things in education is to know how to separate a child from his or her actions.

For example, not to tell the child "you are not okay"; tell him "I do not accept your actions."

An additional example, not to tell the child "I am angry at you." For him or her, this is a rejection, the child feels he is not loved.

Tell him "I am angry at what you have done."

From age seven to the Bat Mitzva or Bar Mitzva

A child needs to be accepted unconditionally.

A child who receives warmth and love unconditionally and equally receives boundaries, is a child who receives security and feels that he or she is loved and will not be abandoned.

From Me to You

Fable – The Glass and the Water

Here is a fable by my dear husband which will illustrate for us the child in us.

The glass = emotion.

The water = child.

If there is a 250cc glass and the amount of water in the glass is 250cc, the influence of the water on the glass will be 100%.

In this case, the child influences the emotion by 100%.

If the glass grows bigger and turns into a pail, the water will not change and will remain 250cc, but the influence of the water on the pail will be only a few percent.

In this case, the child will influence the emotion by a few percent.

If the pail grows to the size of a barrel, the water will remain 250cc, but the water's influence on the barrel will be insignificant.

In this case, the child has no influence on the emotion, but the child remains the same child.

When emotion develops properly, the child will not have influence on the emotion, meaning, in everyday life the behavior will be mature.

But, the child exists and does not change, he or she is yours. Therefore, if you want to, you can use the child within you by choice.

Femininity – Worldly Essence

Dear women, before we understand what femininity is, let us look at the Hebrew word for female, *nekeva*. What do we see in the word *nekeva*?

It is made up of two words in one:

nekev – ba – בה – נקב (*ba* is Hebrew for "in her").

What is *nekev ba*?

It is as if she is all one piercing.

The essence of the piercing is a desire to be filled.

In this way, the female wants to be filled in every respect: in her emotions, in society, economically, and so on…

What is femininity's role?

Femininity's role is to secure the continuity of the chain of life, to care for the next generation, fruit of my loins.

Femininity's role splits into two:

1. Production of offspring
2. Building the nest in which to raise them

How is this done?

Nature's way is to create the state of falling in love.

Falling in love is a hormonal state.

What is the Goal of Falling in Love?

Falling in love has two main goals.

1. First goal – To lead to sexuality in order to create offspring.

How is this done?

Falling in love creates sexual attraction that increases more and more; it creates a strong need to feel closeness and a deep desire to connect.

2. Second goal – To connect the man to the woman, so that they will be able to build the nest for raising the offspring.

How is this done?

Falling in love creates a softening in the emotions.

It provides the option to change behavioral patterns and suit oneself to the other.

It allows us to create a shared life.

For example, like white-hot iron, with a small amount of pressure, it easily changes.

But when it cools, it is difficult to change it.

Falling in love has a limited lifespan.

After falling in love ends, the burning-hot cools down to 25%, 75% turns to love.

Utilization of Time

For this reason, it is important to work in a cooperative way while falling in love. This is the time to change, it is important to utilize the time for heart-to-heart talks, talking about your childhood, about pain, about fears, about weaknesses, about your outlook on life, about your desire, wishes, etc…

All of this allows both partners in the romantic relationship to change in accordance with the other's internal qualities.

What are the feminine traits?

Warmth, passivity, absorption, sensuality, sexuality, presence, containment, softness, domination, and so on.

Living Feminine

Absorption

The feminine woman's power is absorption. A feminine woman who is hurt will not react immediately; she absorbs inside, and only after she calms down she will talk.

For example, if the husband tells a feminine wife, "I want to go out now," even though it does not suit her, the feminine wife will express her desire.

If this does not help, she concedes, let's go. But the husband knows that the silence does not equal her giving up, she will come to talk to him delicately, but this time with the power of her presence; this is passive power.

Therefore, the man respects the feminine woman.

Presence

The feminine woman has a presence that can be seen in her body language, in her standing position, stable sitting position while listening, and in her significant gaze. A feminine woman radiates – I am here and now.

Containment

Feminine women have the ability to contain different and changing situations that happen in life.

Losing Control

A feminine woman who feels she trusts her husband, and has someone to lean on, has no problem losing control and being like water in a glass.

Sexuality

Sexuality in the femininity is the need to bring-up children and care for the next generation.

In femininity, sexuality is a connection out of containment, out of merging, being "one flesh."

Dominates

A feminine woman dominates.

What does it mean to dominate?

To be up-to-date and aware of what is going on all the time, to know what is happening around her.

But through passivity.

For example,

1. I am sitting in a high tower and dominating over all of the valley, everything is revealed to me, I do not need to descend from the tower. But if something is being hidden from me, I get down from the tower and go to the hidden place. The moment I descend the tower

and go to the hidden place I become active. Now, I am controlling and not dominating.

2. When keys fall into a tub of dirty water, we insert a hand to pull them out.

The searching hand controls but the water dominates over the hand.

As Many Details as Possible

It is important for the man to share with his woman as many details as possible regarding how he conducts his life.

The more details the woman knows regarding the way her husband conducts in life, the more she will be dominating and less controlling.

Women, after we have understood the essential traits, which are childishness and femininity, we will now become familiar with the serving traits, which are motherhood and wit.

Motherhood – An Acquired Spiritual Trait

Motherhood is a considerable part of a woman's life.

There are two types of motherhood.

- One type of Motherhood — mother to children.
- Second type of Motherhood — mother to the surrounding environment.

We see that there are two types of mothers, both of whom conduct themselves with motherly traits.

What are the traits of motherhood?

Responsibility, giving, sacrifice, worrying, control, values, morals, observation, empathy, learning from life, learning from experience, education, forgiving, protection, a sense of being on a mission, delaying satisfaction, and so on…

Motherhood – mother to a child

When a woman uses her mothering traits with her children, she functions as a mother, she is in her essence.

Mother to the surrounding environment

When a woman functions using her motherly traits without a choice toward the surrounding environment, meaning, she uses her motherly traits more than the norm, she takes on the role of being the mother of the surroundings.

When a woman functions with her motherly traits out of choice toward the surroundings, she acts in a sensitive way toward her surrounding environment.

When a woman functions with her motherly traits within a romantic relationship, it is very important that the dosage is right.
Motherliness toward a husband needs to be like a spice.
For example, a woman makes sure there will be food that her husband loves.
It is very womanly.
A woman who takes care that he will eat the food –
this is the conduct of a mother to a child.
There are cases in which the woman can function with motherly spiritual traits but who does not have any children.
There can be a woman, who has many children, but who does not have motherly spiritual traits.

Wittiness – An Acquired Worldly Mental Trait

Dear women, it might be that the Hebrew word *shnunit* is not familiar to you, but you can feel at ease.

Indeed, the word *shnunit* is not very well-known in the spoken Hebrew language, but for my dear husband it exists.

The Hebrew word *shnunit*

If we look, in Hebrew, at the word *shnunit*, we will see the root word,

shanun, which, in English, means sharp, or witty.

Shnuniut, or wittiness, is an acquired spiritual trait that is activated by the intellectual sharpness and the excess wisdom.

We will try to understand how when and why, we acquired the wittiness.

The process began in childhood, in three stages.

The First Stage

The first stage is acquired from the age of one and a half years until around the age of seven, where the significant period is from age three until around age five.

During these ages, the girl learns the wittiness opposite the father.

Putting on airs

In the natural development of the girl, the girl learns to put on airs in front of the father, such as "daddy" and so on.

If the father gives in to the girl's airs and gives her the feeling that he melts from her, the girl will grasp it as a strength.

She learns the strength that is in the charming weakness, that over time becomes natural behavior with the romantic partner.

The Second Stage

The second stage is acquired from age seven until around age 14. In these ages, the girl develops wittiness opposite the father and the mother together.

Unclear Speech

The girl has a tendency to speak unclearly. She speaks in half sentences, and does not speak in a direct way. She speaks in unclear phrases, and creates vague communication.

Wittiness in front of society

The girl learns wittiness in front of society, not to be direct, not to hurt, to know how to get along with society without being aggressive; she learns social conduct in preparation for the future, how to manage her home in harmony with the extended family and in front of her friends.

The Third Stage

The third stage is acquired from age 14 until around age 21 – the adolescent years. Here the girl stands opposite her mother, she has a tendency to cope **in front** of her mother; the mother feels that the daughter is competing with her.

The adolescent girl learns with her mother during this period, how to rub femininity with femininity.

It is important that you the mother, maintain the right boundaries, it is important to educate, to cooperate. But it is important not to disrupt the process that the adolescent girl is going through. If there is no awareness, it creates a lot of tension.

For the future, the adolescent girl learns this wittiness in front of members of her own sex.

The Man in Survival State

Women, you should be familiar with the natural primary behavior of the man in the survival state.

How does the man behave when he is in need of help, when he is being threatened?

The man goes into survival mode, the body begins to secrete adrenaline, the muscles in the body begin to work. The body prepares itself for battle.

The Man Feels Threatened

Women, it is important you know, a man also feels threatened by a direct woman.

Why?

A direct woman says things as they are, without observing and seeing her man, whether it is appropriate now.

Without activating thought, how do I tell him? When do I tell him? What do I tell?

We can say that she is lacking in excess wisdom, in wittiness.

What happens to the man?

The man feels he is being attacked.

What happens now?

In the man's subconscious, warning bells ring out: Danger! There is an attack!

The subconscious translates the danger according to the man's primary genes when he went out to hunt, the danger that existed back then of wild predatory animals. Therefore, the subconscious translates the directness into an animal trait from the predator family.

Now, the man enters survival mode and immediately goes into battle.

When a direct woman does not go through the charming process in her childhood with her father, she has not developed her wittiness.

For this reason she reacts under stressful conditions in two ways:

- Acquiescence
- Directness

Wisdom

Dear women, before we get to know wittiness better, it is important for me to show you the primary source for the creation of wisdom.

Therefore, we will come back to our sources and there we will be able to see the creation of the woman's wisdom.

"Then the LORD God made a woman from the rib he had taken out of the man, and he brought her to the man." (Genesis 2, 22)

In the Hebrew bible, the passage begins with the word *Vayiven*. The simple interpretation of the Hebrew word *Vayiven* is *bnia*, or in English, "building."

The sages of the Mishna and the Talmud interpret the word *Vayiven* as *bina*, or, in English, "wisdom."

Conclusion

We can conclude, then, that if wisdom appears in the book of Genesis, the book of creation, how important it is for the woman to use the power of wisdom.

"With wisdom she will build her home"

Woman received wisdom so that she will be able to fulfill her important role of building her home.

When the woman's wisdom connects to her intelligence, the woman receives spiritual insights, and brings them down to the actual act so that she will build her home with wisdom and reason.

What happens under stressful conditions between a woman and her husband?

Excess Wisdom

Here the woman has a need for excess wisdom, there is a need for intellectual sharpness, for wittiness, and for intelligence with an interest.

The Role of Wittiness

Wittiness immediately enters a role. Now, it needs to neutralize as quickly as possible the threat on a romantic relationship, the threat on the family. Her interest now is to do everything to preserve everything that exists, to protect the home she has built.

Wittiness has traits that she uses under stressful conditions.

What are wittiness's traits?

Interest, temptation, initiative, activeness, revealing, seduction, sneakiness, sharpness, determination, eroticism, playing, manipulation, and so on…

Living as Wittiness

Interest

Wittiness knows how to bring the intelligence into the soul, to reason out of a particular interest.
What should I do in the current situation?
If I do this, what will happen?
If I don't do this, what will happen then?

Playing

Wittiness knows how to play her role.
She knows how to bring her husband into the game, without him knowing it, without him feeling it.
Women, you can feel at ease.
The game is only for stressful conditions, it is not a way of life.

Does as he Wishes

Wittiness has the ability to make her man do whatever she wishes and make him think it came from him.

Seduction, Eroticism

Wittiness knows how to get into a role through sexuality, it knows how to bring the seduction, the eroticism out of herself, all for one goal:
- to soften her man and neutralize the battle.

Here is a sweet example from nature.

How does my dear husband say? Everything exists in nature, you only need to look.

For example, the Wagtail is a very nice bird, a wandering bird.

A wonderful thing that my husband learned – the male Wagtails are very territorial, they come to the females, they split up their territories into areas so that nobody will enter their area, and after them come the females. Now they face a problem because all of the territories are occupied.

What do the females do?

They begin producing courtship, just as before the period when they are in heat.

They wag their tails and wings, and the male wagtail responds to the seduction and lets her enter. Now, she is inside.

Women, what is left to say – it is all in your hands!

A Charming Weakness

One of the things that characterize a charming weakness is that the woman knows how to lower herself or raise her man.

When her man is raised,

he can give to her.

This is a weakness of power that is called women's wisdom.

For example, a woman is taking a walk with her husband in the street and they pass a bakery shop. The woman says to her husband, "As a girl I really liked Sabrina cake and since then I have not tasted it."

One should assume that her husband will buy it for her with pleasure. Why?

The woman gave her husband the ability to choose to give to her, to spoil her.

When the woman let her husband choose to give to her, she lowered herself, and he felt that he is above. For this reason, he could give to her.

Women, I want to bring to you a wonderful fable from my dear husband, a very simple fable, but with a large illustration.

The Fable of the Bottle and the Glass

If we take a bottle and a glass, and we want the glass to fill up from the bottle, what should we do?
Naturally, we should lower the glass, or lift the bottle.

If the bottle is not above the glass,
then the bottle will not be able to give to the glass.

Women, in order to receive from your man,
you must bend down,
or lift up your man.
That is power.

From Me to You

The soul's Work

Indeed it is not easy.
It involves a lot of mental work.
It entails overcoming your dignity.
It entails cancelling out your pride,
at times relieving your anger.
It is not simple, but it is the right way to receive from your man.
It is according to the laws of creation.

Wittiness – A Charming Weakness

Introduction

I would like to illustrate for you a graph so that you will be able to see wittiness's movement and the charming weakness's movement on a graph's scale.

Wittiness is an acquired trait that is activated by the intelligence and functions in stressful situations.

Charming weakness is an acquired trait that is activated by the intelligence and functions under normal conditions in life.

How do they move on the scale?

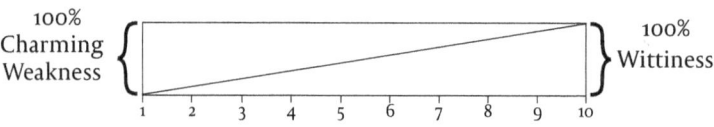

Charming Weakness

We see that at one end there is the trait called charming weakness where the trait that is located at the end is 100% charming weakness.

Wittiness

At the other end, we see the trait wittiness that is located at the end is 100% wittiness.

When you move along the scale on the graph, the relations between charming weakness and wittiness change according to the life's needs.

Femininity is made up of wittiness and charming weakness. The beauty of femininity is that it knows how to play with both, according to the current need.

Dear women, this time as well, I would like to bring in a fable from my dear husband.
The fable is a bit spicy and a bit sweet.
It has come down from the spice shelf,
a trick for keeping the peace at home.

The Fable of the Pepper and the Sugar

Femininity is composed of two opposite materials – pepper and sugar.

The wittiness is the pepper, it is the spicy;

the charming weakness is the sugar, it is the sweet.

Women, when you feel that your husband is a bit sleepy, bring in some pepper, some interest, and watch how he wakes up.

When your husband is a bit bitter, a little bit of sugar won't

do any harm, and watch how the bitter turns to sweet.
You know that:
Excess wisdom – pepper.
And Women's wisdom – sugar.

What is Femininity?

Femininity is one of the traits of the woman's soul that serves the femaleness.

Because the femaleness is essential, passive, and has no executive ability, it needs a performing serving trait.

The serving trait is femininity, this is the "performer," but it appears as passive as the femaleness.

Women, in order for you to understand femininity, I would like to bring in a fable by my dear husband.

This is a fable that was born as a result of his deep observation of nature, a fable that will illustrate in detail and in nuance and subtlety what femininity is.

I am charmed by the fables,

they are so special,

they make us want more…

From Me to You

The Fable of the Flower

Everything for the Butterfly

If you take a good look at a flower, you will be able to see how much executive energy the flower puts in order to attract the butterfly to it.

- How much performance energy does the flower invest in order to produce color?

  The flower does not need the color, it is for the butterfly.

- How much performance energy does the flower invest to produce fragrance?

  The flower does not need the fragrance,

  it is for the butterfly.

- How much performance energy does the flower invest in order to create nectar?

  The flower does not need the nectar, it is all for the butterfly.

We see that in nature, the most similar thing to femininity is the flower.

The flower, like femininity, is very passive – executive.

It invests a lot of energy to produce color, fragrance, and nectar, but the flower looks like femininity, it is the most passive.

Goal

The flower has a goal that is similar to femininity.

The flower's goal is to attract the butterfly to it, in order to make sure there is continuity of the plants in nature.

Femininity has a similar goal in order to attract the male to the female, so that the femaleness will make sure the next generation continues.

How does the flower do this?

The flower has a hidden feminine movement.

The flower has the hidden power of seduction.

With the seductive power of the color, the fragrance, and the sweet nectar, it attracts the butterfly to it and gives the butterfly the feeling, that it is the active one, that it is the initiator.

A Trip in the Field

When you go for a trip in the field, you will be able to see the flower from an additional perspective.

If you look at all the flowers in the field, you will see how colorful and fragrant they are, but, you will also see something strange.

The flowers bloom with all of their beauty even when there is no butterfly around.

From Me to You

If the flowers would bloom only when there are butterflies around, they would become extinct.
What can we learn?

The Creator of the Universe shows us,
that the flower blooms by the power of its female energy.
The flower blooms with charm and beauty,
The flower blooms in all its glory like a crown.
The flower blooms because it is a flower.

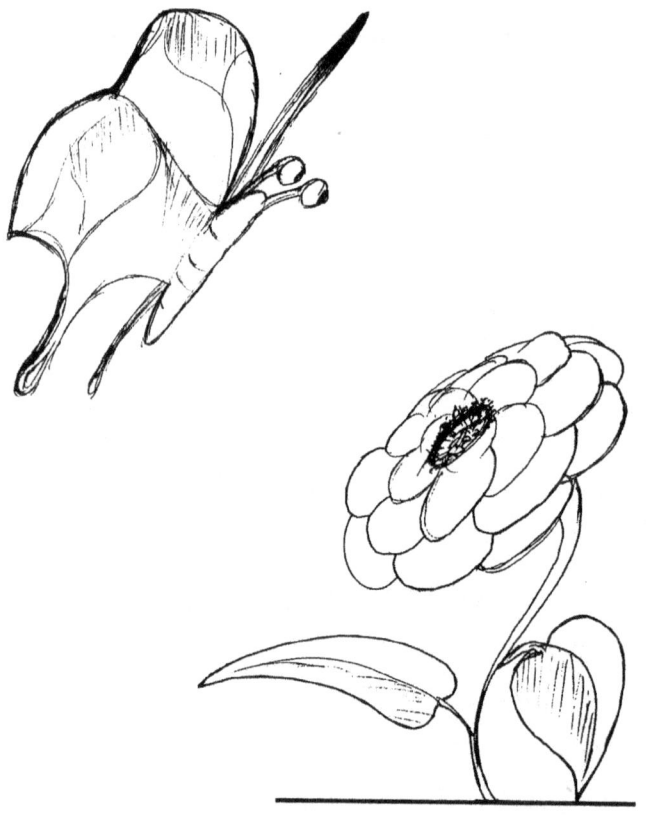

The Charm and Beauty that is in Modesty

Femininity is like a flower.

Women, you need to remember, your hidden feminine movement, is for your husband, with the charm and beauty that is in modesty.

Each and every woman needs to match her special femininity to fit her husband.

Together with this you need to know –
The flower blooms because it is a flower.
You are feminine because you are a woman.
You need to be pampered for yourself, because it makes you feel good.
When femininity becomes your nature, your life, then your man will feel the femininity in you.

Femininity is Me

I want to make my husband want me.
I want to bloom like the flower with all its beauty for my husband.
I want to be my husband's crown.
I want to be "a woman of valor for my husband."
Dear women,

From Me to You

I saw it fit, to end the writing of the book with a prayer, a personal prayer by my dear husband, that has accompanied him and accompanies him on his way… I can say, it accompanies me on my way as well… The name of the prayer is "Poem for the Path."

Poem of the Path

My God give me a **path**
Give me **light** to see the path
Give me **strength** to walk the path
Give me **courage** to stay on the path
Give me **wisdom** to become integrated with the path
Give me **intelligence** to understand the path
Give me **faith** to accept the path
Thank you God for being with me on the path

Seven degrees by which the human being becomes more refined

For the ascent of the soul of
Miriam daughter of Avraham
Of delicate soul and noble spirit

Passed away in good name

י"א בסיון תשנ"ט

ת.נ.צ.ב.ה.

For the ascent of the soul of
Eliyahu son of Yaakov
An innocent and good-hearted man

Passed away in good name

כ"ט אלול תשע"ה

ת.נ.צ.ב.ה.

For the ascent of the soul of
Shlomo son of Avraham
Lover of all beings

Woke up at night to bring bread to his house in the cold and snow.
Worked in the labor camps many days with his head held high.
Gave up material comforts for social justice.

Passed away in good name

ז' אדר תשע"ג

ת.נ.צ.ב.ה.

www.ingramcontent.com/pod-product-compliance
Lightning Source LLC
Chambersburg PA
CBHW060841050426
42453CB00008B/775